RISJ *CHALLENGES*

Red Kayaks and Hidden Gold:
the rise, challenges and value of citizen journalism

John Kelly

REUTERS
INSTITUTE for the
STUDY of
JOURNALISM

UNIVERSITY OF
OXFORD

Contents

Executive summary

Is journalism a profession or a trade? It's a question that has probably only ever interested journalists. It's also a question that, as the 20th century gave way to the 21st, seemed to somehow be beside the point: suddenly you didn't necessarily have to be a journal*ist* to do journal*ism*.

How did that happen? That's what this paper is about.

'Citizen journalism' is the term that has stuck to the practice, which can be very broadly defined as non-journalists doing the things that only journalists used to do: witnessing, reporting, capturing, writing, disseminating. As inelegant as the term 'citizen journalism' is, there's an even uglier one that hints at why this turn of events should have so upended the standard order. That term is 'user-generated content', or—even less pleasant in the mouth—'UGC'.

There is much contained within that phrase to make journalists uneasy. Let's deconstruct it, beginning at the end. 'Content' is a word that calls to mind a commodity, something bland used to fill a hole. 'Generated' isn't much better, suggesting as it does material that's created in some vaguely spontaneous way, untouched by human hands. It is the word 'user', however, that most illustrates how much things have changed. For most of journalism's history users were the people at the end of the production chain: readers, viewers, listeners. News was a broadcast, from one to many. We live in the network age now, where the many can talk to the many, bypassing the one completely.

This has been made possible by technology, hardware and software that provides an alternative to the expensive machinery once necessary to be even the tiniest of media moguls. Users don't have to be users anymore; they can be producers. In fact, the tables have turned so much that the old producers—the newspapers, the TV news operations—are now users.

Today, the mainstream media is continually asking citizens to have their say. And citizens oblige.

Or do they? Some do, certainly. A number of the signature images of the last 10 years have come from non-journalists who happened to be in the right place at the right time—or, more accurately, the wrong place at the right time—with their camcorders, digital cameras or mobile phones at the ready. But overall, the percentages of people who contribute user-generated content are very low, arguably much lower than the furore over the whole issue would seem to warrant—furore over notions of objectivity, transparency and quality.

But supporters of citizen journalism point out that the mere act of generating content can do more than just fill a hole in the corner of a newspaper or a web page. It can improve the journalism itself, by involving in the process people who actually know about, or are affected by, the issue at hand. And it can have a beneficial impact on those content-generating users. It can make them more interested in their communities, it can demystify the political process, it can excite them about the things the best journalism strives to do: explain, crusade, call to account.

It *can* do these things. How often it *does* do them, and for whom, is something worthy of further study. In the meantime, the question 'Should there be citizen journalism?' is beside the point. Journalists must accept that the dynamic has changed. They must see the public as more than an inert, monolithic audience. They must explore new, collaborative ways to tell stories. And they must do all of this on the tilting deck that is today's trade. Or profession.

Introduction: all the news that's fit to make yourself

As 2007 drew to a close an unusual news story captivated the British media and the British public. On 1 December a 57-year-old man named John Darwin walked into a London police station and announced 'I think I am a missing person.' Not only was Darwin, a former teacher and prison officer, a missing person, he was, at least officially, a dead one. Darwin had disappeared in March 2002 while paddling in the North Sea in his red kayak. Thirteen months later a coroner in Hartlepool, County Durham, had issued a death certificate in Darwin's name. Denied by the cruel sea a body to bury, Darwin's wife, Anne, could at least get on with her life, assisted by a £25,000 life insurance settlement.

Five years later, John Darwin reappeared. Darwin's tale smelled a little funny from the start and it wasn't long before the British press started poking holes in it, noting that such floridly cinematic cases of amnesia were rare and that shortly before her husband reappeared Anne Darwin had hurriedly cleared out of her house and emigrated to Panama. The story so bothered one woman—a non-journalist identified only as a 'single mother' who was often 'up late' with her insomniac son—that she did a Google Image search on the words 'John, Anne and Panama'. Up came a photograph of the Darwins from the website of a Panamanian real estate firm, along with a date stamp indicating the photo had been taken in 2006, four years after John Darwin had 'died'.

'I just blinked—and there they were', the woman told the Daily Mirror. 'I rang police in Cleveland. The man on the other end said, "You're joking"!'[1]

[1] 'How Woman Found Darwin Picture', *Mirror* (6 Dec. 2007): www.mirror.co.uk/news/topstories/2007/12/06/how-woman-found-darwin-picture-89520-20210298/

From the comfort of her home, this unnamed woman was able to dip into the near-infinite datastream of the web and pluck out 'news', news that had so far eluded the traditional media. It would be hard to find a better example of how the great engines of news gathering have been changed by the democratizing effects of technology, unless perhaps the woman had emailed a .jpeg of the Darwins to the BBC's 'Have Your Say' website or bypassed the mainstream media entirely and written about her discovery on her blog.

All of these actions and abilities—and many more—fall under the umbrella term 'citizen journalism', which may be broadly defined as non-journalists engaged in activities traditionally performed by journalists. About a decade old, it is a movement that has attracted great attention among those studying and practising journalism. My hope is that this paper will provide readers with a basic grasp of the history and issues involved with citizen journalism, including its similarity to earlier journalistic forms that invited audience input, the claims proponents make for it, the drawbacks critics perceive, the direction it seems to be heading, and the challenges facing the practice as it goes forward.

Perhaps the biggest challenge is this: the health of the Western news media, newspapers especially, is failing faster than new forms of news gathering and revenue can arise to fill the gap. This dire landscape makes discussions of user-generated content seem almost beside the point. And yet it seems certain that the impulses underlying the rise of citizen journalism are here to stay, ensuring that citizen journalism will, in some form, be a part of whatever form of media is standing after the current shakedown.

1. Technology makes every citizen a publisher

The rise of citizen journalism is primarily a result of technology.[2] By that I don't mean that there are no laudable impulses behind the citizens who embrace or practice it, just that in the past there were very few ways that people could make known beyond the sound of their own voices facts they had uncovered or opinions they held. To disseminate information broadly meant making ferociously expensive capital investments in technology: printing presses, television transmitters, radio towers. As a result, the 20th century was the age of the wealthy press baron. It was also the age of the mass media, 'mass' because in order to recoup high upfront costs, owners needed to spread their product to as many people as possible.[3]

The media may have been 'mass' in terms of the (hoped for) audience at the receiving end, but it was not mass in terms of messengers at the creation end. A newspaper is a finite receptacle with a limited amount of space for content. So, too, is an evening news broadcast. In nearly all cases this content is created by professional journalists, individuals who by dint of education or experience are considered 'qualified' for their jobs. And so the mass media's diffusion model can be described as 'from the few to the many': few reporters and editors, employed by few owners, engaged in the

---

[2] OECD, *Measuring User-Created Content: Implications for the 'ICT Access and Use by Households and Individuals' Survey* (30 Jan. 2008), at www.oecd.org/dataoecd/44/58/40003289.pdf, lists 'four drivers' of user-generated content: (1) technological (e.g. more widespread broadband uptake, new web technologies which facilitate the posting, rating and aggregation of data); (2) social (e.g. demographic factors, attitudes towards privacy); (3) economic (e.g. increased commercial involvement of internet and media firms in the hosting of user-created content); (4) legal (e.g. rise of more flexible licensing schemes).

[3] In non-market economies or repressive societies, the press is controlled by the state, a situation just as restrictive to broad dissemination of news.

business of broadcasting or publishing to many readers, viewers or listeners. As Yochai Benkler writes: 'When the economics of industrial production require high up-front costs and low marginal costs, the producers must focus on creating a few superstars and making sure that everyone tunes in to listen or watch them. This works reasonably well as long as there is no better substitute.'[4]

The internet provides, if not a *substitute* medium, then a *parallel* one, a low-cost distribution mechanism that is newspaper delivery truck, paper boy, and radio and TV transmitter all in one. With this network in place what was next needed to approximate journalism were some of the tools journalists use. These came in the form of hardware, such as compact digital cameras, camcorders and camera-equipped mobile phones; and software, including blogging software (the equivalent of the typesetting and pagination systems of the print media), image- and sound-editing software, and search engines such as Google. As prices for these tools came down, and internet broadband penetration increased, more and more people could take advantage of them.

As Benkler writes: 'The material requirements for effective information production and communication are now owned by numbers of individuals several orders of magnitude larger than the number of owners of the basic means of information production and exchange a mere two decades ago.'[5]

Journalism's 'failures' as a catalyst for action

The stage was set for the rise of citizen journalism. But the tools and the network weren't enough.[6] It was also necessary that citizens feel motivated to take on roles traditionally performed by the media. It was here that the media itself played a role, although perhaps not in the way it would have liked. The media has never been perfect and journalism is prey to the same shortcomings as any industry, its practitioners as fallible as those in any profession. But journalism's unstated aim—to tell the truth without fear or

[4] Yochai Benkler, *The Wealth of Networks: How Social Networks Transform Markets and Freedom* (Yale University Press, 2006), 55.
[5] Ibid. 4. He also notes that the internet 'is the first modern communications medium that expands its reach by decentralizing the capital structure of production and distribution of information, culture and knowledge'. Ibid.
[6] On the determinism of technology and how inevitable an outcome is based on technology, see Benkler: 'All other things being equal, things that are easier to do are more likely to be done, and things that are harder to do are less likely to be done. All other things are never equal. ... Neither deterministic nor wholly malleable, technology sets some parameters of individual and social action. It can make some actions, relationships, organizations, and institutions easier to pursue, and others harder. In a challenging environment—be the challenges natural or human—it can make some behaviors obsolete by increasing the efficacy of directly competitive strategies.' Ibid. 17.

favour—elevates it in such a way that failing to live up to that standard can be especially damaging.

Over the last decade readers, viewers and listeners have been treated to a series of well-publicized journalistic mis-steps. In 2003 *New York Times* reporter Jayson Blair admitted he had fabricated and plagiarised details in dozens of stories, including those involving sniper killings in the Washington area and US soldiers wounded in Iraq. Also that year British journalist Andrew Gilligan told a BBC radio audience that Tony Blair's Labour government had 'sexed up' a dossier involving Saddam Hussein's military capabilities, an accusation that was deemed untrue after an extensive government inquiry.

Failures such as these helped underscore a growing conviction that the news media couldn't be trusted, a belief that the media, if not actively corrupt, was at best mediocre. While trust is a difficult metric to measure,[7] a 2008 Ipsos MORI poll put journalists in a virtual tie for last place among 16 'trusted professions' in Britain, with just 18 per cent of respondents answering that they would generally trust journalists to tell the truth.[8] Things are much the same in the United States. A 2007 poll by Sacred Heart University in Connecticut found that fewer than 20 per cent of those surveyed said they believed all or most US news media reporting, down from 27 per cent four years earlier. Researchers also found that an increasing number of people believed the media tried to influence public opinion and policy.[9]

Researchers at the Pew Research Center's Project for Excellence in Journalism noted that in 2007 'Majorities of Americans continued to say that journalists are often inaccurate (55%), do not care about the people they report on (53%), are biased (55%), one-sided (66%) and try to cover up their mistakes (63%). Those sentiments, all more prevalent than in the 1980s, have become entrenched.'[10]

Journalist and professor Eric Alterman in the *New Yorker* wrote: 'Vastly more Americans believe in flying saucers and 9/11 conspiracy theories than believe in the notion of balanced—much less "objective"— mainstream news media.'[11]

---

[7] For the most developed recent argument on this, see Adrian Monck, with Mike Hanley, *Can You Trust the Media?* (Icon Books, 2008).

[8] www.ipsos-mori.com/content/polls-07/doctors-still-top-the-poll-as-most-trusted-profess.ashx The poll was commissioned by the Royal College of Physicians and doctors ranked as the most trusted profession. Pollsters were about in the middle, behind 'the ordinary man/woman in the street' and above civil servants.

[9] www.sacredheart.edu/pages/20786_americans_slam_news_media_on_believability.cfm

[10] http://www.stateofthenewsmedia.org/2008/narrative_special_attitudes.php?cat=1&media=13

[11] Eric Alterman, 'Out of Print', *New Yorker* (25 Mar. 2008).

Such sentiments were intertwined with another belief: that the so-called mainstream media's control of information—the stories it chose to cover, the way it chose to cover them, the relative weight it gave to different spokespeople or groups—was unnecessarily restrictive. There arose a feeling—hard to quantify but especially prevalent among some of those most comfortably positioned at the cutting edge of digital technology—that despite its high calling the media was little different from any other industry that had grown big, gotten complacent and lost touch with its customers.[12] The media's gatekeeper function was increasingly obsolete in a world where there suddenly were no fences. As an editor at CNET.com, a popular technology website, put it: 'Big media has been laying down the rules for a long time, and there's no doubt they've abused their power, lost our respect, and alienated an increasingly tech-savvy generation.'[13]

This, then, was the atmosphere when the news media bungled one of the biggest stories of the last 30 years: the US-led invasion of Iraq. Especially in the United States, journalists were accused of not exercising sufficient scepticism toward the claims made by President Bush and those in his administration regarding Saddam Hussein's weapons of mass destruction.[14] What had been a belief that the mainstream media was increasingly irrelevant was joined by a belief that it was actually complicit—either through inattention, incompetence or outright bias—in a disastrous foreign policy.[15] When *New York Times* editor Bill Keller delivered the Hugo Young Memorial Lecture in November 2007, he

---

[12] Advocates of this viewpoint 'generally agree that commercialization and professional hubris have reduced the ability of mainstream journalism to perform this role. And so they frame collaborative newsgathering as a way of overcoming this loss.' David Ryfe and Donica Mensing, 'Doing Journalism Together: Experiments in Collaborative Newsgathering', paper presented at the Future of Newspapers Conference, Cardiff, 2007.

[13] Molly Wood, senior editor at CNET.com, quoted in David Kline and Dan Burstein, *Blog!: How the Newest Media Revolution is Changing Politics, Business, and Culture* (CDS Books, 2005).

[14] No less a figure than Scott McClellan, former spokesman in the Bush White House, embraced this viewpoint, writing in his memoir: 'If anything, the national press corps was probably *too* deferential to the White House and to the administration in regard to the most important decision facing the nation during my years in Washington, the choice over whether to go to war in Iraq. The collapse of the administration's rationales for war, which became apparent months after our invasion, should never have come as such a surprise. ... In this case, the "liberal media" didn't live up to its reputation. If it had, the country would have been better served.' *What Happened: Inside the Bush White House and Washington's Culture of Deception* (Public Affairs, 2008), 156–7.

[15] The pre-war reporting by *New York Times* reporter Judith Miller, and her reliance on Ahmed Chalabi as a source, came in for special criticism. See James C. Moore, 'Not Fit to Print', *Salon* (27 May 2004): http://dir.salon.com/story/news/feature/2004/05/27/times/

included a telling line: 'I'm constantly surprised by the presumption of bad faith when people talk about our business.'[16]

Keller was alluding to something that puzzles many mainstream journalists with any history in the profession (that is, those who can remember a time before the internet): how can so much of the public believe that journalism is untrustworthy at a time when, to reporters and editors, quality journalism seems 'better'—more responsible, more even-keeled—than it has ever been before?[17] While some veteran journalists believe that current practices suffer when compared to a 'golden age', they often forget that staffs were typically smaller then, there was less newshole, owners were just as meddlesome, journalists were not as well educated, and the same prejudices that infected society as a whole were apparent in stories.

What's different is that readers then had nothing to which they could compare the journalism that was delivered to them. The internet changed that, making 'news' something more than what could be purchased at the news stand or pulled in by an antenna. Today's journalists are not sloppier than yesterday's. Rather, readers are more demanding. Technology has given them choice in other areas of their lives and they seek it in their media. Readers can now communicate much more easily with one another, comparing what they see in the mainstream media and what they encounter outside the media.

It was not just that some observers saw mainstream journalism as flawed.[18] It was a feeling that some of the failings of journalism were due to the way its practitioners often walled themselves off from the rest of society, seldom explaining how they worked, reluctant to demystify what was, to many, an opaque process.

---

[16] Hugo Young Memorial Lecture, delivered 29 Nov. 2007. Full text at www.guardian.co.uk/media/2007/nov/29/pressandpublishing.digitalmedia1 Keller went on to say: 'That is in some measure the fault of our own shortcomings, the well-publicised examples of journalistic malfeasance, the episodes of credulous reporting in the prelude to the war in Iraq, the retreat of some news organisations from serious news into celebrity gossip, and so on. It also reflects the fact that we live in cynical times, in a clamorous new media world of hyperventilating advocacy.'

[17] Note this exchange between Alicia C. Shepard and former *Washington Post* editor Ben Bradlee in *American Journalism Review*, 17 (Mar. 1995): *AJR: Obviously, you and Post Executive Editor Len Downie have different strengths. Can you talk about how the Post is different today than it was under you? BCB: I can't really. I think the Post is infinitely better run. It's administered a lot better. That didn't turn me on, that kind of administration. Downie is fantastic at it. Loves it.*

It would be interesting to study the public's reaction to the 'professionalism' of journalism, as it evolved from what might be called the Bradlee model—charismatic figures prone to big gestures—to the Downie model: sober figures with a more technocratic approach. In short: do readers want better run newspapers?

[18] Or, as David Ryfe and Donica Mensing put it, 'Advocates of collaborative newsgathering then, begin from the premise that mainstream journalism has lost its way.'

2. Antecedents in civic journalism

The belief that an underserved audience could take matters into its own hands was not entirely unprecedented. The rise of the alternative press in the 1960s stemmed from a similar impulse: we will do for ourselves what the news media will not do for us. But the cost of producing and distributing even the most basic sort of newspaper or magazine was beyond the means of all but the most devoted enthusiasts.

Thirty years later it was the mainstream news media that experimented in this arena. Deciding that covering the news without input from the people most affected by it was shortsighted, and concerned that civic life was suffering because of an unengaged public, some newspapers embraced a movement known as 'civic journalism'.

Civic journalism, or 'public journalism', arose in the United States in the early 1990s and was characterized by 'involving readers both in the news-making process and the use of news. The backbone of civic journalism is polling of readers, the arranging of public meetings, and newspapers framing the scope of reader involvement in a way that produces stories.'[19] Surveys were commissioned, focus groups were convened, town-hall meetings were held. Readers were invited to discuss their concerns about such issues as crime, government, development and education; to confront candidates and elected officials; and to take part in setting the journalistic agenda—at least in an advisory, if not a participatory, way.[20] This was a step towards the current model of citizen journalism.

[19] J. Nip, 'Exploring the Second Phase of Public Journalism', *Journalism Studies*, 7/2 (Apr. 2006), 216.
[20] Civic journalism did not escape some of the criticisms later aimed at citizen journalism. Consider this sentence from *Editor and Publisher* (20 May 2002): 'Civic journalism earned its decidedly mixed reputation because it too often seems to involve timorous reporting followed by community meetings led by editors acting so earnestly you fear that any minute they will take out a guitar and lead everybody in a chorus of "Kumbaya."'

'The difference between then and now', write David Ryfe and Donica Mensing, 'is that new technologies are available and that, after several more years of difficulties, journalists may be more receptive to the idea of changing their relationship to audiences.'[21]

Changing the relationship: the early years

If the traditional relationship between the news media and its audience was one of producer and consumer, the new relationship was not quite so rigid. Steve Paulussen, Ari Heinonen, David Domingo and Thorsten Quandt wrote: 'Rather than talking about media producers and consumers occupying separate roles, we might now see them as participants who interact with each other according to a new set of rules that none of us fully understands.'[22]

It should not come as a surprise that for a movement so dependent upon technology, it was in the technological arena that the first experiments with this new relationship took place. In October 1999, Johan J. Ingles-le Nobel, the deputy editor of *Jane's Intelligence Review*, a journal of 'threat analysis', commissioned an article on cyberterrorism. Unhappy with the draft he received, he posted the piece on Slashdot, a technology website popular with self-confessed 'nerds'. Ingles-le Nobel reasoned that some of Slashdot's readers would be familiar with the topic and able to offer useful feedback. The odds were good that Slashdot's readers would collectively know more than any single author could. 'For our part, we'll make an article based on your replies,' he wrote.[23]

Ingles-le Nobel's decision was not met with universal acclaim and the response from some quarters presaged the arguments that were to come later over citizen journalism. On his blog Robert Cringely, a technology columnist for PBS, wrote: 'This is an interesting idea but ultimately flawed, I think. The only way to write the news is to write the news. You have to do it the best that you can then take the heat, because the censorship of the nerderati is still censorship. That's why newspapers make corrections.'[24]

Cringely's mindset is familiar to anyone who worked at a newspaper at the time. Far from a fluid, malleable product, news was more akin to a chunk of steel or a new car: finished when its maker said it was finished.

[21] David Ryfe and Donica Mensing, 'Doing Journalism Together'.

[22] Steve Paulussen, Ari Heinonen, David Domingo and Thorsten Quandt, 'Doing it Together: Citizen Participation in the Professional News Making Process', paper presented at the COST 298 Conference 'The Good, the Bad and the Unexpected: The User and Future of Information and Communication Technologies', 23–25 May 2007, Moscow.

[23] http://slashdot.org/article.pl?sid=99/10/04/0836212&tid=99

[24] www.pbs.org/cringely/pulpit/1999/pulpit_19991007_000626.html

Involving the audience raised the same risks as interfering in the annealing process or tampering with the assembly line. Jane's editors weren't concerned. After reading through more than 250 comments on the cyberterrorism article, Ingles le-Nobel decided to spike the original story and write a new one based on the observations of Slashdot's users.[25]

The bedrock metaphor for this kind of citizen journalism is *news as a conversation* as opposed to *news as a lecture*. As early proponent Dan Gillmor explained:

> *Big Media ... treated the news as a lecture. We told you what the news was. You bought it, or you didn't. You might write us a letter; we might print it. ... It was a world that bred complacency and arrogance on our part. It was a gravy train while it lasted, but it was unsustainable.*
>
> *Tomorrow's news reporting and production will be more of a conversation, or a seminar. The lines will blur between producers and consumers, changing the roles of both in ways we're only beginning to grasp now. The communication network itself will be a medium for everyone's voice, not just the few who can afford to buy multimillion-dollar printing presses, launch satellites, or win the government's permission to squat on the public's airwaves.*[26]

A journalist in South Korea had had a similar epiphany. Oh Yeon-Ho had worked for an alternative monthly magazine and thus had an outsider's view of journalism. He was convinced that Koreans were dissatisfied with their country's traditional media and that they were eager to make their opinions known. In 2000 he started the website OhmyNews.com, taking as its slogan 'Every citizen is a reporter.' It was, he said, a motto both empowering and humbling; empowering because it suggested that citizens could be more than passive receptors, humbling because it reminded professional reporters that they now faced competition from an unlikely source. By 2003, OhmyNews had nearly 27,000 citizen contributors, their submissions—some 200 a day—overseen by a staff of 53. It was turning a profit and its coverage of Korean politics was credited with helping elect Roh Moo-hyun as president.[27]

---

[25] http://features.slashdot.org/article.pl?sid=99/10/07/120249&mode=nocomment

[26] Dan Gillmor, *We the Media* (O'Reilly Media Inc., 2006), p. xxiv.

[27] Yeon-Jung Yu, 'OhmyNews Makes Every Citizen a Reporter', *Japan Media Review* (17 Sept. 2003): www.japanmediareview.com/japan/internet/1063672919.php. Interestingly, Oh said in this interview that OhmyNews did not support Roh's candidacy, just that it wrote about it more than the mainstream press and that it did this because of his appeal to young people who, it would seem, would be natural OhmyNews contributors and readers.

Understudies in a starring role: citizens capturing the news

It was a series of tragedies, however, that illustrated in Britain and the United States just how motivated and journalistically productive the audience could be, and cemented the belief that citizen journalism in some form could have a role to play in covering even breaking news.

The news media covered the terrorist attacks of 11 September 2001 with saturation images on television and in-depth stories in newspapers and news magazines. What the media of the time couldn't be expected to do was give voice to anyone who wanted to rage, mourn, dissect, comment or share emotions about the attacks in a public way. Blogs, however, could do that. With a blog—an updatable online diary, usually with the ability for readers to leave their own thoughts and reactions—anyone could distribute their thoughts across the internet.[28]

The Asian tsunami of 26 December 2004 showed another aspect of citizen journalism. Western news organizations weren't in place to cover the disaster in Indonesia and Thailand. Tom Glocer, the head of Reuters, wrote, 'For the first 24 hours the best and the only photos and video came from tourists armed with telephones, digital cameras and camcorders. And if you didn't have those pictures, you weren't on the story.'[29] Most of the early photos and videos of the destruction were provided by amateurs, including vacationers who just happened to be in the affected areas when the waves swept ashore.

Similarly iconic pictures appeared on front pages seven months later, after Islamist terrorists detonated bombs on London's public transportation system, killing 52. The 7 July bombings marked a turning point for citizen journalism in the United Kingdom. The BBC received 22,000 emails and text messages, 300 photos and several video sequences. 'That was the day the phenomenon of "user-generated content" (UGC) or "citizens' journalism" came into its own in Britain, as members of the public took over the roles of photographers and news correspondents,' wrote BBC media correspondent Torin Douglas. 'Dramatic stills and video sequences from passengers on the Tube trains led the BBC Six O'Clock

---

[28] According to Pew Research, in the days following the Sept. 11 attacks, nearly one-third of all American internet users 'read or posted material in chat rooms, bulletin boards or online forums'. Quoted in Shayne Bowman and Chris Willis, *We Media: How Audiences are Shaping the Future of News and Information* (Media Center at the American Press Institute, 2003, pdf available at: www.hypergene.net/wemedia/weblog.php).

[29] Tom Glocer's Blog, 2006: http://tomglocer.com/blogs/sample_weblog/archive/2006/10/11/98.aspx Quoted in Glenda Cooper's 'Anyone Here Survived a Wave, Speak English and Got a Mobile? Aid Agencies, the Media and Reporting Disasters since the Tsunami', 14th Guardian Lecture, presented at Nuffield College, Oxford University 2007.

News bulletin, the first time such material had been deemed more newsworthy than the professionals' material.'[30]

Citizen journalism had arrived. But what exactly did that mean?

---

[30] 'How 7/7 "Democratised" the Media', http://news.bbc.co.uk/1/hi/uk/5142702.stm See also Richard Sambrook, 'Citizen Journalism and the BBC', *Nieman Reports*, 59/4 (Harvard, Winter 2005), 13.

3. Citizen journalism: definitions, motivations, benefits, criticisms

What is citizen journalism?

'Citizen journalism' is the term by which this phenomenon or practice is most widely known but it is by no means the only one.[31] Other terms have entered the lexicon, among them: user-generated content, user-created content, participatory journalism, audience material, 'we media', collaborative journalism, community journalism, pro-am collaboration, grassroots journalism, open-source journalism, crowd-sourced journalism, interactive journalism, networked journalism, network publishing, bridge media and 'random acts of journalism'. Whatever it's called, perhaps the best definition comes from *We Media: How Audiences are Shaping the Future of News and Information*, a 2003 report by Shayne Bowman and Chris Willis. To them citizen journalism refers to the 'act of citizens playing an active role in the process of collecting, reporting, analyzing and disseminating news and information'.[32]

Citizen journalism is defined more by *what* it is than by *where* it is. That is, it can exist within the framework of a mainstream media outlet and it can exist on its own, a posting by an independent blogger or an

---

[31] In this age of immigration controversy, there are some political objections to the term 'citizen journalism': "'We are uncomfortable with the term 'citizen journalism,'" said Todd Wolfson, 35, a doctoral candidate at the University of Pennsylvania and one of the organizers of the Media Mobilizing Project in Philadelphia. "We prefer the term 'community journalism.'"' Quoted in Noam Cohen, 'Journalism in the Hands of the Neighborhood', *New York Times* (10 Mar. 2008). Available at www.nytimes.com/2008/03/10/technology/10link.html
[32] Bowman and Willis, *We Media*. See also OECD's *Measuring User-Created Content*, 14, which defines 'user-created content' as: 'i) content made publicly available over the Internet, ii) which reflects a certain amount of creative effort, and iii) which is created outside of professional routines and practices.'

image on a photo-sharing website. Also, the level of complexity of a user-generated product can vary. It can be a self-produced video uploaded to YouTube and it can be a comment posted at the end of an online newspaper story. Broadly speaking, user-generated content can even be something other than content. It can be the exercise of influence, influence news consumers have seldom had before.

Citizens can express their interests and desires with what are known as user-controlled recommendation and linking portals. Websites such as Digg.com and Reddit.com allow users to nominate and vote on other sites that they have found interesting. The more votes those sites receive, the more prominently they are displayed on the Digg or Reddit home pages. Users interested in a quick survey of what is attracting like-minded web users can simply go to Digg.com or Reddit.com for what amounts to a leader board of currently popular sites. Similarly, the 'most read' or 'most emailed' stories on a traditional news media website illustrate the tastes of readers.

There are other ways the audience is contributing. Hyperlocal websites are online repositories of news and information unique to a specific town or neighbourhood, with content largely provided by unpaid contributors. These websites may be created by existing news companies, by entrepreneurs or by activists.[33]

Stand-alone citizen journalism websites such as NowPublic.com invite users to submit stories, photos, videos and audio files, or to augment the offerings of other NowPublic users with their own observations or media. In 2008 cable news giant CNN launched a website called iReport.com which allows viewers to directly upload video to the site, without the intervention of any human editors.[34]

Crowdsourcing is the act of distributing the reporting function across many people.[35] The hope is twofold: first, that a news outlet's great corpus of readers might include experts well-equipped to tackle a complex subject

---

[33] The Knight Citizen News Network lists around 800 such sites in the USA: www.kcnn.org/citmedia_sites

[34] www.nowpublic.com and www.ireport.com. Both sites explicitly reference the gatekeeping function of traditional media and set themselves up in opposition to it: '[At NowPublic] we're not a bunch of elite reporters and you don't have to be either. We're crowd-powered news. That means it's fresh and unpackaged.' (Welcome video at http://www.nowpublic.com/getpublished.) 'At CNN we live for news. We love talking about it. And we know that there's a whole lot more to it than what you see on TV or read on your favorite Web site. So we've launched an independent world where you, the iReport.com community, tell the stories we're not used to seeing.' (www.ireport.com/about.jspa;jsessionid=232AF6961CDA3CD9C413552DB3E2FBD7)

[35] *Wired* writer Jeff Howe defines crowdsourcing as 'the act of taking a job traditionally performed by a designated agent (usually an employee) and outsourcing it to an undefined, generally large group of people in the form of an open call.' (http://crowdsourcing.typepad.com)

(as in the Slashdot cyberterrorism example), and second, that an information-dense topic might be broken down into manageable chunks by the combined efforts of many eyeballs. Examples include the thousands of pages of documents related to the firing of US attorneys by the Justice Department posted by the Talking Points Memo Muckracking website. After Hurricane Katrina, the Fort Myers News-Press in Florida posted Federal relief data online and asked readers to look over it. In Britain, the *Guardian* has posted documents related to the BAE corruption case [36] and to the issue of MPs' expenses, inviting its readers to dig through the 70,000 PDF documents released by the House of Commons.[37]

A wiki, a continuously updatable web page to which nearly anyone may contribute, is another form of crowdsourcing. Wikipedia.org, the online, volunteer-written encyclopedia, is the best-known example. Wikinews.org is an attempt to apply the model to journalism, with volunteers posting observations, links and source material related to breaking news stories in an attempt to create a 'neutral point of view'.[38]

[36] http://tpmmuckraker.talkingpointsmemo.com/ Fort Myers example from Charlie Beckett, *SuperMedia: Saving Journalism So it Can Save the World* (Blackwell Publishing, 2008), 54.
[37] http://www.guardian.co.uk/politics/mps-expenses
[38] www.wikinews.org. See also Paul Bradshaw, 'Wiki Journalism: Are Wikis the New Blogs', presented at the 2007 Future of Journalism Conference, Cardiff (http://wikijournalism.pbwiki.com). Bradshaw describes wikis as a platform which can contain journalism, not a form of journalism *per se*.

4. How the mainstream media adopted and adapted

The mainstream media moved slowly to integrate some of these aspects into their products. In a 2008 paper Alfred Hermida and Neil Thurman[39] identified nine generic formats that British newspaper websites have put in place to encourage contributions from the public:

- Polls: Topical questions where readers are asked to make a multiple choice or binary response.
- Messageboards: Areas of the site that allow readers to engage in threaded online conversations or debates on topics often initiated by readers.
- Have your says: Similar to messageboards, but these features are in response to questions posted by journalists, who select, edit and publish some comments.
- Comments on stories: Reader comments at the bottom of an article.
- Q&As: Interviews with journalists or invited guests, with questions submitted by readers.
- Blogs: Posts laid out in negative chronological order, authored by one or more individuals, often associated with a set of interests or opinions, frequently including links to external websites.
- Reader blogs: As above, but authored by readers, not staffers.
- Your media: Galleries of photos, video and other media submitted by readers and vetted by journalists.
- Your story: Readers are asked to send in stories that matter to them, edited by journalists for publication on the website.

[39] A. Hermida and N. Thurman, 'A Clash of Cultures: The Integration of User-Generated Content within Professional Journalistic Frameworks at British Newspaper Websites', *Journalism Practice*, 2/3 (2008), 343–56.

In their 2008 report 'UGC @ the BBC', Claire Wardle and Andrew Williams outlined five different types of what they dubbed 'audience material' in use at the public service broadcaster: audience content (including audience-submitted footage), audience comments, collaborative content, networked journalism and non-news content.

These are useful frameworks for 'user-generated content', or UGC, the type of citizen journalism most widely practised by the mainstream media. The term speaks to the new way in which many mainstream media organizations view the audience. No longer mute recipients of news, readers can now provide material for publication, from comments on news stories to photographs that may themselves be news.

It is important to note that many of these methods can exist inside or outside the formerly walled garden of the mainstream media, or straddle the wall. The press borrows or appropriates forms it believes will strengthen its product, attract an audience or allow it to compete with newer types of media already using those techniques.[40] Blogs are a good example of this.

A word about blogs

Blogs are a problematic entity to study in the overall context of citizen journalism. Most of the early attention about the audience's shift from receiver to producer was focused on blogs. The bitterness of those early debates still obscures the landscape.[41] Blogs vary as to subject matter but what most have in common is a publishing schedule that isn't tied to anything other than their creators' energy, a way for readers to easily add comments and a reverse chronology of past entries.

Blogs encompass everything from meticulously researched investigative stories to random musings on pets, celebrities and celebrities'

---

[40] Growth of UGC between Apr. 2005 and Nov. 2006: blogs jumped from 7 to 118. Comment on stories jumped from one to six. 'Have your say' grew more slowly, from three to five. From Hermida and Thurman, 'A Clash of Cultures'.

[41] Often when blogs are discussed by British journalists the Drudge Report is mentioned. And yet, strictly speaking, the Drudge Report isn't a blog. It is an aggregation of websites, typically comprising links to mainstream media web pages (www.drudgereport.com). Even the scoops that Matt Drudge is occasionally credited with—e.g. the Bill Clinton/Monica Lewinsky affair and Prince Harry's service in Afghanistan—are usually the work of mainstream journalists whose spiked stories are leaked to him or whose obscure stories are publicized by him. The early ire over Drudge among mainstream journalists probably stemmed from his apparent contempt for *being* a journalist, while wrapping himself in the trappings of one. Nevertheless, news executives relish being linked from Drudge, since it can substantially raise traffic.

pets. The vast majority are not what might be termed 'newsy'.[42] Those that are, however, can be especially bracing and many adopt a tone that worried (and still worries) some in the mainstream media. There was a fear that blogs existed somehow outside the objective journalistic sphere. Newspapers were slow to adopt blogs, seeing in their sometimes freeform and unedited style something antithetical to traditional journalism.[43] What is clear is that it is impossible to pigeonhole blogs. Some produce material that is sober, credibly sourced and relatively objective. Others shoot from the hip, trading in gossip and innuendo. But even most of the bloggers behind even the most outrageous blogs don't wish for the death of the mainstream media, nor do they see themselves as a replacement for it. In a survey of 300 political bloggers worldwide by Michael Maier, a minority (37 per cent) saw themselves as 'journalists'. Most preferred to define themselves as 'commentators' (72 per cent) or 'analysts' (67 per cent):

> *Our survey also contradicts another predominant prejudice, namely, that bloggers want to destroy the old media. Only a tiny fraction (7 percent) thought that blogging was going to 'replace old media,' and 4 percent saw no interaction between blogging and the old media at all. The overwhelming majority (83 percent) saw blogging as 'complementary to old media.' Nor do they feel they really threaten the media: 26 percent saw themselves as a threat, but 74 percent thought that they 'add value to the old media.' Of course, they want to be unique: 78 percent say that they are 'covering what old media misses.'[44]*

Blogs are often seen as the symbol of citizen journalism and it is telling that most US and UK newspapers eventually embraced a form many once thought was toxic.

[42] The Pew Internet and American Life Project found in 2006 that most bloggers wrote about issues other than news. Nearly four in 10 (37%) said they blogged mainly about their 'life and experiences', with issues of public life (11%) cited as the second most popular topic area. Just 5% said they concentrated primarily on news and current events. (http://www.pewinternet.org/PPF/r/186/report_display.asp)

[43] There's another reason why newspapers may have been slow to embrace blogs at first: newspaper reporting was often the target of bloggers' ire. Newspaper editors may have resisted the appeal of the form, seeing it as something that was only good for spewing vitriol. Austrian journalist Michael Maier: 'Many in the old media would define the relationship as parasitic, with the notorious blogger, in his pajamas, working from the basement of his home, taking the news produced by the old media and passing it through his own distorting system.' *Journalism without Journalists: Vision or Caricature?* Discussion paper #D-40 in the Joan Shorenstein Center on the Press, Politics and Public Policy series, John F. Kennedy School of Government, Harvard University, Nov. 2007, p. 11.

[44] Ibid. This is in line with findings in the 2006 Pew Internet and American Life Blogger Callback Survey. Note also that, according to the Pew study, bloggers tend to be more interested in the news than other internet users.

Why do it? Assessing motivations

Dr Johnson wrote 'No man but a blockhead ever wrote, except for money.' Money is certainly a motivation for some citizen journalists. It is an entrepreneurial impulse, one that's understandable to mainstream publishers who, as philanthropic as they may be, must pay attention to the bottom line. Other recognizable reasons citizens try their hands at some form of online journalism include the desire to express opinions, to learn from their reporting and to inform others of what they've learned. Prolific blogger Glenn Reynolds wrote: 'I think the impulse among humans to share opinions is pretty well hardwired, meaning that as long as weblogs aren't expensive, people will happily do it at a loss.'[45] But the unique characteristics of the digital media inspire other motivations.[46] They include the following.

For recognition or the enhancement of one's reputation

In his book *The Long Tail* Chris Anderson posits that the power of search engines makes it possible to be successful in ever-smaller creative niches. Customers, his argument goes, will be able to find you, despite how narrow your appeal may be. Some of those who inhabit the web's nether reaches are interested in reaping something other than profit:

> *Down in the [long] tail, where distribution and production costs are low (thanks to the democratizing power of digital technologies), business considerations are often secondary. Instead, people create for a variety of other reasons—expression, fun, experimentation and so on. The reason one might call it an economy at all is that there is a coin of the realm that can be every bit as motivating as money: reputation. Measured by the amount of attention a product attracts, reputation can be converted into other things of value: jobs, tenure, audiences, and lucrative offers of all sorts.*[47]

[45] Glenn Reynolds, instapundit.com, Frequently Asked Questions:
www.instapundit.com/extra_archives/2002_06.php
[46] A nice set of motivations for contributing to news aggregating sites is described in Hsing Wei, 'The Hype vs. Reality vs. What People Value: Emerging Collaborative News Models and the Future of News', Harvard University's John F. Kennedy School of Government
(http://citmedia.org/learn/surveys/collaborativenews.htm). The paper also explores barriers to contributing.
[47] Chris Anderson, *The Long Tail: Why the Future of Business is Selling Less of More* (Hyperion, 2006).

For exposure

Here again, people's motivation can be different from those in the pre-digital world. Tim Lu writes: 'The exposure culture reflects the philosophy of the Web, in which getting noticed is everything. Web authors link to each other, quote liberally, and sometimes annotate entire articles. ...And at the center of this exposure culture is the almighty search engine. If your site is easy to find on Google, you don't sue—you celebrate.'[48]

For activism

Some people are moved to start a blog, comment on a story or send in a photo because they want to bring about a certain outcome. They are activist citizen journalists who make no qualms about the subjective fashion in which they approach their stories. 'They are writing articles to change the world, not to earn money,' said Oh Yeon Ho, founder of *OhmyNews*.[49]

To engender a sense of community

The internet allows groups of like-minded people to find each other and coalesce around common interests. Citizen journalism helps these individuals communicate with one another.

For the joy of creation

For some, the lure of citizen journalism is not connected to attracting readers or effecting change. The lure is simply to go through the act of putting their thoughts on a screen.[50] It is the rush familiar to any journalist who pleased himself or herself with a well-turned phrase or a cogent observation. Chris Willis and Shayne Bowman write: 'Traditional media tend to understate the value of participation journalism, holding that comments, reviews and content created by "amateurs" provide little value to their mass audience. As such, they are missing the inherent psychological value of the creative process to the individual.'[51]

That is the central attraction of citizen journalism, and indeed the attraction of so much digital technology: it elevates the user from an observer to a creator, whether that creation is a blog posting, a hurriedly snapped news photo, a song assembled on a laptop, or a home movie uploaded to YouTube.

---

[48] Tim Wu, 'Leggo My Ego: Google Print and the Other Culture War', www.slate.com/id/2128094
[49] Quoted in Anderson, *Long Tail*.
[50] According to the Pew Internet and American Life Blogger Callback Survey: 'Three in four bloggers (77%) told us that expressing themselves creatively was a reason that they blog. Younger and lower-income bloggers were more likely than other groups to give this as a reason to blog. Similarly, most bloggers (76%) say that they blog to document their personal experiences and share them with others. Younger users were among the most likely to say that they blog to document and share their lives.'
[51] Willis and Bowman, *We Media*, 41.

What there is to love: assessing benefits

Citizen journalism's supporters see many benefits in this ability to create and post content free from the former strictures of traditional journalism.

- *It brings experts into the reporting process so that stories can be more accurate and nuanced.* A common criticism levelled against journalism is that it often only scratches the surface of issues. Confronted with a deadline, a reporter must quickly cram himself with knowledge then spew it onto the page. By necessity he is a jack of all trades, if also quite often a master of none. Supporters of citizen journalism argue that inviting readers to contribute to reporting improves the end result. As Dan Gillmor puts it:

  > *It boils down to something simple: readers (or viewers or listeners) collectively know more than media professionals do. This is true by definition: they are many, and we are often just one. We need to recognize and, in the best sense of the word, use their knowledge. If we don't, our former audience will bolt when they realize they don't have to settle for half-baked coverage; they can come into the kitchen themselves.*[52]

- *It makes possible the coverage of events that the mainstream media might otherwise miss.* Citizens with a viewpoint or agenda that differs from that of the mainstream media can unearth news that might be overlooked.[53] A story can happen even if a reporter isn't there to witness it. Especially in remote areas or in countries with repressive governments, citizen journalists might be the only ones poised to get the facts.
- *It can save money.* By enlisting the help of unpaid volunteers, news organizations can supplement their offerings with user-generated content. This could allow them to redirect their resources at a time of

[52] Gillmor, *We the Media*, 111.
[53] As Reich describes it: citizen journalism is 'expected to fill numerous lacunae that the mainstream media has ignored and compensate the general public for some of the myriad shortcomings of the press'.

declining circulation, advertising and profits.[54] Also: website operators are fond of successful user-generated content programs because such programs are 'sticky'. They encourage loyalty and multiple visits to the website, increasing traffic and, potentially, ad revenue.

- *Through blogs especially, it can influence the news agenda or 'resuscitate' stories the mainstream media might have let die.*[55] Most journalists understand in some deeply intuitive sense what makes something a story in the first place and what developments justify follow-up stories. Resource restrictions—newshole, reporter and editor time, lack of access—often dictate both the initial story and later incremental articles. This can be less of an issue with citizen journalists, whose motivations may be more personal, less profit-driven, and indeed, may border on the monomaniacal. Also, coverage that would seem unacceptably excessive in a traditional newspaper is more acceptable on a blog, with its often confrontational style and different standards of objectivity. Finally, the internet can have a metastasising effect. As more and more blogs link to an article, or to each other, a story can have a life beyond the traditional news cycle. Occasionally the mainstream media feels compelled to follow up on stories that appeared first on blogs or that were championed by bloggers.[56]

- *It can demystify the journalistic process.* Journalism can seem opaque to the general public. Both the *policies* of journalists—how stories are chosen; the ethics of the profession—and the *process* of journalism— the nuts and bolts of reporting—have rarely been communicated to

---

[54] See Wolfgang Schweiger and Oliver Quiring, 'User-Generated Content on Mass Media Web Sites: Just a Kind of Interactivity or Something Completely Different?', paper presented to the 55th annual conference of the International Communication Association (2005). They identify the following benefits of UGC. (1) It *is low-cost content* and thus can help to fill sites with content quite economically. (2) UGC delivers *added value* to active and passive users. The active users are pleased to have a platform for their communication to the public or to other users. Passive users may find it interesting to read what others think. (3) Presenting some kind of a democratic platform for public debates can *improve the image of a media product*: the most important dimensions are probably tolerance against other opinions, transparency and credibility. (4) UGC can be used as a kind of low-cost market research—an attempt to *learn about their audience's needs, preferences and expectations* in order to create a more user-oriented media product.
[55] The most commonly quoted examples of this include the debunking by bloggers of CBS News' story about George Bush's National Guard records (www.washingtonpost.com/wp-dyn/articles/A34153-2004Sep19.html) and the blogosphere uproar over House Speaker Trent Lott's remarks in support of Sen. Strom Thurmond in 2002 (www.wired.com/culture/lifestyle/news/2002/12/56978).
[56] It's unclear how often blogs lead the news agenda. Levon Lloyd, Prachi Kaulgud and Steven Skiena compared 500,000 blog postings with 66 daily US newspapers over five weeks. They decided that 'there is no clear trend of blogs leading the news or news leading the blogs. A nearly equal number of entities fall on both sides.' 'Newspapers vs. Blogs: Who Gets the Scoop?', paper presented at the 2006 Association for the Advancement of Artificial Intelligence, Spring Symposium Technical Report SS-06-03 (AAAI Press, Menlo Park, CA).

readers, viewers and listeners.[57] Now that citizens can try some forms of journalism on their own—and now that more and more mainstream media outlets are inviting user participation—they will inevitably understand more of the machinery. Gillmor writes: 'If this goes well, we'll move into a new era of media literacy and what we might call news activism.'[58] Charlie Beckett, director of POLIS at the London School of Economics, writes: 'By sharing the process with the public it offers a new relationship of greater transparency and responsibility. [Journalism's] primary function is still to chase the stories that dominate our public agendas, but stories that are more honestly told. And by involving the public it also forces the consumer to take responsibility for their part in the news media market.'[59]

- *It can build a sense of community, increasing the understanding of, and participation in, civic life.* This is the benefit that the most ardent proponents of citizen journalism hope for. To them, journalism has failed at its most basic task: covering society and its institutions in a way that prepares citizens to exercise their rights, make informed decisions and contribute to the political process. Axel Bruns writes:

> *The decline of popular participation in Western democracies has been long lamented. As we have seen here, on the other hand, public participation in other collaborative projects is growing, and it is possible that this newfound enthusiasm for making an active contribution to the common good can also translate to a reinvigoration of political processes.*[60]

Bruns isn't alone in hoping that bringing citizens inside the circus tent of journalism will inspire more participation in civic life. A citizen who covers his community as a quasi-journalist may have more commitment to it. David Ryfe and Donica Mensing write:

> *By increasing the stock of human and social capital in the community, democracy will be benefited in both direct and*

---

[57] Not that there was any reason to. I disagree with those who believe the mainstream media has been trying to keep something from citizens, or been involved in some conspiratorial deception with the elites that it covers. That's not to say that journalists haven't been guilty of ignoring a desire among readers to have the process made more transparent.
[58] Gillmor, *We the Media*, p. xviii.
[59] See Beckett, *SuperMedia*, 62.
[60] Axel Bruns, 'The Future is User-Led: The Path towards Widespread Produsage', presented at 'perthDAC 2007: The Future of Digital Media Culture', 7th International Digital Arts and Culture Conference (http://snurb.info/node/719)

indirect ways. Indirectly, it will benefit from more cohesion and trust among community members. Directly, it will benefit by increased civic and political activity.[61]

Those, then, are the claims made by citizen journalism's boosters. Posed against them are some pointed criticisms. Zvi Reich writes: '[T]he very question of whether ordinary citizens are at all capable of producing news is the subject of an on-going theoretical and practical dispute, which can be divided into three schools of thought: the naysayers, the well-wishers, and the mixed school.'[62]

We'll leave aside the notion that the dispute over citizen journalism divides into three schools of thought and instead propose that criticisms of citizen journalism generally fall into two categories: *moral/ethical/quality* criticisms and *practical/technical/administrative* ones.

What there is to hate: moral criticisms

The main criticism levelled at citizen journalism is a simple one: it isn't very good. That's the argument made by Andrew Keen in his book *The Cult of the Amateur: How the Democratization of the Digital World is Assaulting our Economy, our Culture, and our Values*. Keen frames his objections in almost primatological terms: untrained people trying to commit acts of journalism (or movie-making or music) are like the metaphorical infinite number of monkeys banging away on an infinite number of typewriters. Most of what they produce will be garbage. The occasional gem will be almost accidental. Keen writes that, despite its lofty goals, democratisation of the type exemplified by citizen journalism

> [is] *undermining truth, souring civic discourse, and belittling expertise, experience and talent. [It] is threatening the very future of our cultural institutions. ... What the Web 2.0 revolution is really delivering is superficial observations of the world around us rather than considered judgment. The information business is being transformed by the Internet into the cacophony of a hundred million bloggers all simultaneously talking about themselves.*[63]

[61] Ryfe and Mensing, 'Doing Journalism Together'.
[62] Zvi Reich, 'A Matter of Accessibility: Comparing the Sourcing Practices of Citizen and Mainstream Journalists', paper presented at the Future of Newspapers Conference, Cardiff, 2007.
[63] Andrew Keen, *The Cult of the Amateur* (Currency/Doubleday, 2007), 16.

This is the sort of attitude guaranteed to inflame citizen journalism's most ardent supporters. To them, Keen embodies the elite, stifling mindset that has poisoned traditional journalism and made it ripe for toppling. But his argument does get to a fundamental issue: what is a journalist? Are journalists, by dint of their training, different from non-journalists? Or is a journalist anyone who creates something approaching journalism?

The issue is one of standards. For the most part, a newspaper or a TV news operation has some level of legitimacy, a result of its history, its perceived professionalism or authority, its standards or ethics, the trust its users place in it.[64] This legitimacy may be unknown with a blog or user-created site and, indeed, there have been cases where individuals have gamed the system, deliberately posting material they know not to be true.[65] In this new world, old notions of trust may not apply.[66]

This issue is slightly different for user-generated content that nestles in the bosom of the mainstream media. Here the issue is also one of legitimacy. Including the work of citizen journalists may legitimize that content, but it also runs the risk of *delegitimizing* the 'legacy' content created by professional journalists. Critics argue that when integrated into a traditional media product, citizen input has the potential to harm the established brand, by making possible the publication of material that is of poor quality, confusing or incorrect. The fear is that things such as outrageous reader comments in the staid confines of a newspaper website could make other users wonder exactly what it is they're reading. Write Hermida and Thurman of their interviews with Fleet Street newsroom managers: 'The potential that UGC has to damage a newspaper's brand remained a prevailing concern among some editors.'[67]

An example: a story in April 2008 in the *Daily Mail* reported that in a medical trial, up to a third of girls offered an inoculation against the human papilloma virus that causes cervical cancer refused the shot, casting doubt

[64] 'It is often difficult to know who is posting information on the Internet and what their motives are, but newspaper journalists are named and identified with an organisation which has set standards': interview with *Guardian* editor Alan Rusbridger in Sean Scanlon, 'News as Conversation', Reuters Institute, 2006.
[65] In Feb. 2008, not longer after CNN unveiled its iReport.com citizen journalism portal, Kyle MacRae uploaded a dramatic photo of a forest fire to the site. MacRae, a journalist and the founder of user-generated photo site Scoopt, identified it as a fire in Scotland that broke out during a 'wild haggis' hunt. It was, in fact, a well-known photo from a 2000 Montana forest fire (www.scunnered.com/?p=9). Interestingly, users of iReport quickly debunked the image.
[66] See Beckett, *SuperMedia*, 59. 'In the digital era the Internet will provide vast amounts of communication and informational data and activity. But if it is not trusted then it is not news journalism.'
[67] Hermida and Thurman, 'A Clash of Cultures'.

on whether a national rollout of the vaccine would succeed.[68] After the story was posted on the paper's website, a reader identified as 'Maggie, Oxford' commented that the US Food and Drug Administration is 'well aware' that HPV has not been linked to cervical cancer, that some girls have died within hours of receiving the vaccine and that drug companies are more interested in profits than in health. Proponents of online comments might argue that this is exactly the sort of dialogue that a newspaper can sponsor on the web. Critics might argue that it leaves a mistaken impression in readers' minds. (The vaccine is seen as safe by medical experts.) Does the newspaper have an obligation to moderate or edit such comments, or rebut them completely?[69]

A third moral/ethical/quality criticism is that an embrace of user-generated content has the potential to skew the overall perception of a story. In the past, reader reaction to a story was confined to the letters page. Published missives were selected and edited by newspaper employees. This arguably was subject to its own selection bias, but most likely the end-result roughly reflected the mix of stories and viewpoints originally published in the paper. The path from reader's keyboard to online comment page is less restricted than that travelled by a letter to the editor. A burst of online activity from one quarter or another has the possibility to misrepresent public sentiment on that issue. Peter Horrocks, head of television news at the BBC, wrote: 'We cannot just take the views that we receive via e-mails and texts and let them dictate our agenda. Nor should they give us a slant around which we should orient our take on a story.'[70]

Related to this is the fact that those who actively participate in the citizen journalism opportunities of mainstream media sites represent only a fraction of total users. For example, it is estimated that the people who contribute to the Have Your Say section of the BBC's news website

---

[68] *Daily Mail*, 'Anti-Cancer Jab Shunned: One in Three Girls Refuses Vaccine to Guard Against Cervical Virus' (24 Apr. 2008):
www.dailymail.co.uk/pages/live/articles/news/news.html?in_article_id=561827&in_page_id=1770
[69] This issue was spotlighted 19 May 2008 when a story in the *Guardian* criticised the MyTelegraph section of the *Telegraph's* website for hosting a blog from a British National Party candidate. Sean Dodson, 'Platform for Free Speech ... or Hate?', www.guardian.co.uk/
media/2008/may/19/pressandpublishing.telegraphmediagroup In his blog, *Telegraph* communities editor Shane Richmond pointed out that the *Guardian's* Comment Is Free section includes questionable comments: http://blogs.telegraph.co.uk/technology/shanerichmond/may08/comment-is-free-perhaps-too-free.htm See also:
http://blogs.telegraph.co.uk/technology/shanerichmond/may08/that-comment-is-free-argument-again.htm and
http://blogs.journalism.co.uk/editors/2008/05/28/guardian-publishes-string-of-anti-telegraph-stories-cue-spat/
[70] Peter Horrocks, BBC The Editors blog, 'Value of Citizen Journalism' (7 Jan. 2008).
www.bbc.co.uk/blogs/theeditors/2008/01/value_of_citizen_journalism.html

represent roughly 1 per cent of the total number of site visitors.[71] A story might receive 1,000 emailed comments, but 100,000 people may have read it.[72]

Also at issue is who those citizens/commenters are. A self-selected group of technologically savvy individuals—motivated, perhaps, by extremes of opinion—may not be the most representative of society as a whole. Nor can it be guaranteed that citizens will even avail themselves of the opportunity to interact.[73]

Concerns aren't confined to user-generated content herded under the mainstream media umbrella. User-recommendation sites such as Digg.com have been criticized for aggregating material that, as a whole, isn't reflective of the news—at least as defined by the traditional news media. A study of three user-recommended sites by the Pew Center for Excellence in Journalism found that the 'news agenda of the three user-sites was markedly different from that of the mainstream press. Many of the stories users selected did not appear anywhere among the top stories in the mainstream media coverage studied. And there was often little in the way of follow-up. Most stories on the user-news sites appeared only once, never to be repeated again…'[74] Critics could argue that basing one's awareness of the world on user-generated sites could offer a skewed vision of reality.

Perhaps the most detailed examination of a mainstream media outlet's involvement with user-generated content was conducted by researchers from Cardiff University, who spent a year interviewing BBC journalists and managers, analysing BBC content and surveying audience members.

---

[71] Email with Vicky Taylor, Editor, Interactivity, British Broadcasting Corporation. 21 May 2008.

[72] This is consistent with what observers have dubbed 'participation inequality'. As summarised by Jakob Nielsen, an expert on human–computer interaction: 'In most online communities, 90% of users are lurkers who never contribute, 9% of users contribute a little, and 1% of users account for almost all the action.' Accessed at www.useit.com/alertbox/participation_inequality.html

[73] Witness a plea on the blog of Jeff Howe, an author who is quite literally writing the book on crowdsourcing. Howe had been posting drafts of his book chapters online and inviting readers to poke holes in them: 'The problem: Too few comments and, more to the point, too few commenters. This is a shame because I'm confident that given enough eyeballs this limited but, to my mind, significant act of crowdsourcing would constitute a nifty new model of book publishing.' Quoted at www.digidave.org/adventures_in_freelancing/2008/05/critique-on-cro.html

[74] Project for Excellence in Journalism, 'The Latest News Headlines—Your Vote Counts', http://journalism.org/node/7493. Coverage of the war in Iraq accounted for 10% of all articles in the traditional press that week, but across the three user-news sites that PEJ studied, it made up just 1% of all stories. In keeping with my thesis that this movement is born out of technology, I note that Digg and Del.icio.us users selected technology and science stories out of proportion to the mainstream press. 'In short, the user-news agenda, at least in this one-week snapshot, was more diverse, yet also more fragmented and transitory than that of the mainstream news media. This does not mean necessarily that users disapprove or reject the mainstream news agenda. These user sites may be supplemental for audiences. They may gravitate to them in addition to, rather than instead of, traditional venues. But the agenda they set is nonetheless quite different.'

The report, 'UCG @ the BBC', catches the corporation at a unique moment. Substantial investment had been made in soliciting user-generated content and an impressive and smoothly functioning UGC hub had grown to employ more than two dozen people. At the same time there was a feeling that the BBC had not arrived at a firm consensus on how the material best fit into its overall structure.[75]

The Cardiff researchers found a savvy audience that saw value in user-generated content. A majority of the people surveyed thought this content should be vetted by professional journalists. Many felt that the various arms of the BBC too frequently begged for audience opinion.[76] They favoured targeted calls for contributions over general pleading. Some focus group participants said they were reluctant to contribute, fearful that they would be lumped in with the uninformed and inarticulate postings that seemed to characterise much of the commentary. Specific content-related requests—as opposed to broad calls for opinion—were valued more.

For their part, BBC editors said it was easy to get swamped by the influx of audience material and that journalists must guard against believing it is in any way representative of the public at large. Journalists also felt that UGC was invaluable for identifying sources and that it seemed a foundation upon which to build more ambitious collaborative programmes.

Making it work: technical criticisms

Then there are what might be called the *technical* criticisms of citizen journalism. Who is responsible for user-generated material published on a mainstream media website? Do unmoderated comments expose a newspaper or TV news operation to legal action if a user posts something libelous or defamatory? Or, as in the United Kingdom, does the mere act of editing shift responsibility to the news organization?[77]

---

[75] C. Wardle and A. Williams, 'UGC @ the BBC: Understanding its Impact upon Contributors, Non-Contributors and BBC News' (16 Sept. 2008, www.bbc.co.uk/blogs/knowledgeexchange/cardiffone.pdf). Of those Britons surveyed, 17% said they had submitted material to a newspaper, 9% to a radio programme discussing news and current affairs, 7% to a TV programme discussing news and current affairs and 4% to a dedicated news website.

[76] At this point in this ponderous paper you no doubt need a laugh. A fitting one can be found in a skit done by the British comedy team Mitchell & Webb, who skewered the BBC's constant 'Have Your Say' requests on their Radio 4 programme. Says Mitchell, after begging listeners to comment on a particular story: 'You may not know anything about the issue, but I bet you reckon something. … Let us enjoy the full majesty of your uninformed, ad-hoc reckon.' Accessed at www.youtube.com/watch?v=tyl9wltqQZ4

[77] That's the case with Britain's Press Complaints Commission. It has oversight of articles printed in newspapers and those articles that appear on newspaper websites. It does not, however, respond to complaints about user comments on websites, unless those comments have been edited by the newspaper staff in some way.

These concerns underscore another criticism: the cost savings of citizen journalism can be illusory.[78] Publishers eager to encourage user-generated content as a way of saving money may find that not to be the case. Reduced costs of acquiring material may be offset by the increased costs of editing that material. Likewise, moderating comments to remove abusive language is labour-intensive. So too is wading through submissions looking for worthwhile material to highlight in some way.

Publishers or editors hoping to be involved in collaborative efforts with citizen journalists may find that their volunteers are more citizen than journalist. In other words, not only do citizen journalists lack traditional skills, but as they are typically uncompensated they have little incentive to learn or to rework their contributions.[79] This is in some ways a rebuke to Keen's argument that the web has us drowning in dross. Rather than too much content, usually it's a case of not having enough. Both UGC critics and supporters would do well to keep in mind that the number of amateur journalists is exceedingly small. The Cardiff University BBC study found that only 5 per cent of Britons surveyed would contact a news organization if they witnessed a large factory fire and knew that emergency services had been contacted. 'A further 14% *would* take a photo but only 6% said they would send it to a news organisation. The remaining 8% would take a photo but *not send* it to a news organisation.'[80]

Another problem is the reluctance of some journalists to engage with citizens in the way required by this form of journalism. There are several reasons for this. Journalists generally tend to be slow to adopt new forms of technology and, as discussed above, this is a technology-inspired movement. Also, journalists' work habits typically involve structured releases of official information. Pieter Ugille and Steve Paulussen write:

---

[78] P. Bradshaw, 'Wiki Journalism: Are Wikis the New Blogs?', paper presented at the Future of Newspapers Conference, Cardiff, 2007. See also Paulussen *et al.*, 'Doing it Together'. The paper compares citizen participation in several European countries. Of Germany, the authors write: 'Still, there are some doubts about the true reasons for the adoption of user generated content in mainstream online media. It is not unlikely that the developments are labeled by the managements as "democratic", "pluralistic" and "trendy", while they are primarily trying to lower the costs for professional editors by using "free" content happily provided by users.' Another issue is that advertisers might not want to be associated with user-generated content or be willing to pay as much to nestle among it as they would for professionally produced content.
[79] Reich, 'A Matter of Accessibility'.
[80] C. Wardle and A. Williams, 'UGC @ the BBC'. Of course, one might expect these numbers to increase as it becomes easier to contribute.

One could argue that the rather limited use of user-generated content in the professional news production has to do with the fact that professional journalists somewhat routinely rely on a number of official, institutionalized sources of information. Looking at user-generated content (blogs, forums, etc.) or interacting with users do not seem to be part of the daily routine activities in the newsroom.[81]

Finally, for a phenomenon so clearly born out of advances in technology, over-reliance on that technology can be problematic. User-generated images of a natural disaster, blogs about a military coup, mobilephone video of a plane crash—these things can only be seen by the wider world when the technology works. Said Reuters editor David Schlesinger: 'The Internet was key to getting stories and images out [of Burma], but the generals know that by turning off the Internet they could black out the country again. Technology gives, control of technology takes away.'[82]

---

[81] P. Ugille and S. Paulussen, 'Moderation, Conversation and Collaboration? Organisational Implications of Citizen Journalism Projects in Professional Newsrooms', paper presented at the Future of Newspapers Conference, Cardiff, 2007.
[82] David Schlesinger, 'Journalism in the Age of Innovation', lecture to Reuters Institute for the Study of Journalism (17 Oct. 2007). For more on crackdowns on bloggers, see Reporters Without Borders, Worldwide Press Freedom Index 2007 (www.rsf.org/article.php3?id_article=24025).

5. The larger issues

So what should we think about citizen journalism? Does it help or hinder the news media? Does it increase democratic participation and strengthen the social fabric? In short, is it good or bad?

One place to start might be by examining how citizen journalism is different from mainstream journalism. Unfortunately, not much quantitative research has been done in this area. Some research suggests that citizen content produced jointly with mainstream media tends to be 'softer and more focused on personal and community life, more rooted in commentary, and less concerned with day-to-day hard news such as politics and crime'.[83]

Ben Gurion University's Zvi Reich did a study comparing the sourcing practices of citizen journalists with those of professional journalists.[84] Reich's findings say as much about the shortcomings of mainstream journalism as they do about the potential (and, indeed, the shortcomings) of user-generated content. He found that there was not a great disparity in the number of sources consulted by mainstream and citizen journalists: 2.52 per story for professional journalists versus 2.18 for amateurs. Where there *were* differences were in the sorts of sources, the sorts of stories and the genesis of stories. While stories in the mainstream media were largely the result of official disbursements of information, citizen journalism story

[83] See Jeremy Littau 'Content Differences for an Online Newspaper Site and its Citizen Journalism Publication', paper presented to the Association for Education in Journalism and Mass Communication meeting, Washington, DC, 2007. 'The findings have implications for those who believe newspapers serve a critical democratic function; that is that the news contained in the pages help people be informed about public policy in local, regional, and national government.' But Littau studied only one newspaper, *The Bakersfield Californian*, and its citizen-produced, reverse-published online component, *The Northwest Voice*.

[84] Reich, 'A Matter of Accessibility'.

choice was largely defined by what Reich terms 'serendipitous encounters and idiosyncratic choices of lay people as well as their inability to access better-positioned sources'.

The citizen journalists Reich studied were not able to rely on traditional sources of information: press releases, official statements, news conferences and the like. Sources were not inclined to perceive them as a forum where the newsmakers would like to appear. Thus they were kept out of the loop of routine source-controlled exchanges. This forced the citizen journalists to initiate story contacts more frequently than professionals did. Reich found that citizen journalists relied on human sources less often than mainstream journalists (they were fond of harvesting information from the web), though those human sources they did use were more likely to be ordinary citizens as opposed to elites. Citizens were also more likely than the mainstream media to initiate stories, especially in the news discovery phase, and to engage their sources face to face rather than on the telephone.

This provides support for two somewhat contradictory viewpoints. Reich's findings embolden those who see in the mainstream news media an entrenched journalism dependent on being spoon fed information from official sources. They lend credence to the opinion that mainstream reporters won't (or can't[85]) get out of the office and talk to citizens. But the findings also support those who argue that citizen journalism can't (or mustn't) replace mainstream journalism. Interestingly, however, the citizen journalists Reich studied *wanted* access to official sources, but because they worked for non-established organizations they were denied it. They were also hampered by their limited journalistic know-how, their high turnover rate and the generally underfunded and weak nature of their organization's structure. Reich writes: 'In light of the above, citizen news organizations have little choice but to adopt an "inclusive" editorial policy, which basically invites anyone to write about anything at anytime.'

As for the quality that supposedly differentiates citizen journalism sites from their mainstream counterparts—their actual openness—the research is surprising. A Pew Center for Excellence in Journalism study of 64 US citizen journalism sites found that most exerted strong control, not allowing uploading of material by visitors:

Blogging allows citizens to open up the marketplace of ideas and contribute their opinions and ideas. Other than allowing visitor

---

[85] See Nick Davies, *Flat Earth News* (Chatto & Windus, 2008). One of his central arguments is that smaller newspaper and wire service staffs are required to produce more and more content, reducing the likelihood that reporters will be able to speak face to face with an actual person.

comments about posted material, however, the majority of people running the sites analyzed here tended to be strong gatekeepers.[86]

The 2008 US presidential election

If citizen journalism was whelped by disaster—through such events as the London Tube bombings and the Asian tsunami—it reached adolescence during the 2008 US presidential campaign. Here was an opportunity to apply aspects of citizen journalism—crowdsourcing, blogging, user-generated video—to an important story unfolding on a relatively predictable schedule. It was also a story that to many of citizen journalism's supporters illustrated the most severe shortcomings of traditional journalism. Critics argued that, when it came to politics, issues and policy were neglected in favour of substanceless horse-race coverage, insiderish examinations of campaign strategy and an infatuation with candidates' images.[87]

The most visible player in the mix of new outlets dedicated to covering the campaign was OffTheBus.net, a website launched in the summer of 2007 by Jay Rosen of New York University and Arianna Huffington, founder of The Huffington Post. The website's name was chosen to differentiate its amateur contributors from those who were 'on the bus': professional media reporters who travelled with the campaigns, enjoying what critics perceived as cosy relationships with the people they were covering. In her introduction to the new site, Huffington decried 'what happens when reporters hop on board the same bus — and the Conventional Wisdom gets passed around like a joint at a Grateful Dead concert'.[88]

Promised Huffington: 'Our disparate mix of citizen reporters won't be part of the mainstream pack covering the campaigns — and will come at it from a wide range of different angles and perspectives, adding a new dimension to campaign journalism.'

OffTheBus.net started with about 300 unpaid contributors. By November 2008 and the election more than 12,000 people had

[86] Project for Excellence in Journalism's 'Report on Citizen Journalism Sites in the State of the News Media' (www.stateofthenewsmedia.com/2008).
[87] Mike Gruszczynski, 'Comparing Apples and Blogs: Presidential Campaign Framing Among Blogs and the Mainstream Media', presented at the 2009 meeting of the Midwest Political Science Association (www.allacademic.com//meta/p_mla_apa_research_citation/3/6/0/3/9/pages360390/p360390-1.php).
[88] 'OffTheBus: HuffPost's Citizen Journalism Project Gets a Name, and Gets Rolling' (19 June 2007, www.huffingtonpost.com/arianna-huffington/offthebus-huffposts-citiz_b_52712.html).

participated, including 1,700 writers. Volunteers attended campaign events, accompanied canvassers and pored through candidate financial records. These activities were not necessarily dissimilar from those the mainstream media might take. But OffTheBus claimed that its contributors differed in scope—thousands of eyeballs—and in where they looked for stories. The website's editors pronounced themselves more interested in ideas that bubbled up from the grassroots than in messages imposed by the campaign. Most startling for many traditional journalists, OffTheBus contributors were not bound by long-standing journalistic notions of objectivity. This was considered a benefit, not a drawback. Who knew more about the details of the campaign process than those who were involved in it in a partisan way?[89]

OffTheBus gained most of its notoriety from two incidents involving a regular contributor named Mayhill Fowler, a 61-year-old non-journalist from California who paid her own way around the country following candidates. A Barack Obama supporter and Obama campaign donor, in April 2008 Fowler was at a California fundraising event that was closed to the press but not, Obama's campaign later said, 'off the record'. Speaking to an audience of wealthy Californians, Obama said of low-income Pennsylvania voters: 'it's not surprising then they get bitter, they cling to guns or religion or antipathy to people who aren't like them or anti-immigrant sentiment or anti-trade sentiment as a way to explain their frustrations'.

Fowler's digital recorder was running. She was troubled by Obama's remarks—and by the prospect of reporting them. She was worried how they would make her candidate look. But she felt it was an important story and after working with her editor on how to contextualise what Obama had said, her story was posted on OffTheBus under the headline 'Obama: No Surprise That Hard-Pressed Pennsylvanians Turn Bitter.'[90]

Two months later, Fowler caught the attention of Bill Clinton during a campaign event in South Dakota. The former president, and spouse of candidate Hillary Clinton, had recently been the subject of a critical article in *Vanity Fair* magazine. As Clinton shook her hand, Fowler asked: 'Mister President what do you think about that hatchet job somebody did on you in *Vanity Fair* … ?' Clinton responded with what Fowler, in her OffTheBus post, called 'a salty stream of epithets', describing the article's author,

---

[89] A. Michel, 'Get Off the Bus: The Future of Pro-Am Journalism', *Columbia Journalism Review* (Mar./Apr. 2009). The stories and blog postings of OffTheBus contributors were not totally unfiltered. Michel led a small staff of editors who reworked leads, edited copy and worked with the writers.
[90] 'Obama: No Surprise that Hard-Pressed Pennsylvanians Turn Bitter' (11 Apr. 2008, www.huffingtonpost.com/mayhill-fowler/obama-no-surprise-that-ha_b_96188.html).

former *New York Times* reporter Todd Purdum, as 'sleazy', 'dishonest' and a 'scumbag'.[91]

After both instances Fowler came under withering attack for blurring the line between citizen and journalist. She had gained entry to Obama's California event by virtue of her position as a contributor to his campaign. She had not prefaced her question to Clinton with the words, 'I'm a journalist'. Some in the mainstream media chastised Fowler for breaking the 'rules'. As Ed Pilkington summarised in the *Guardian*:

> *The debate rages on over both the Fowler stories. They have raised big questions about the limits of the press. Where does the line now lie between public interest and individual privacy? They have thrown in the air the journalistic rule book, and nobody knows exactly what has landed. And they have brought to the surface huge issues about the interaction between traditional media and politics. Is the relationship an essential part of democracy, or a buddy system verging on the corrupt?*[92]

Among those rejecting the validity of the rulebook was Jay Rosen, the co-founder of OffTheBus, who in two lengthy posts on his blog deconstructed the events and urged journalists to question the status quo. To Rosen, a show of objectivity was not preferable to a pledge of transparency. He wrote: '"Trust me because I mask my true feelings about the matter" is not an inherently better way to journalize or gain cred. "Trust me because I show you what my true feelings on the matter are …" can also work.'[93]

What was sometimes lost in the furore was the fact that both sets of remarks—Obama's and Clinton's—were newsworthy; that while Fowler may not have been a 'proper' journalist she did what one would hope a proper journalist would do: publish; and that neither the Obama nor Clinton campaigns complained about Fowler's right to do just that. The two episodes were also reminders that in the age of the citizen journalist 'off the record' was losing much of its meaning.

The candidates were eager to capture a bit of user-generated energy themselves. To a greater or lesser extent (greater among Democrats, lesser

[91] 'Bill Clinton: Purdum a "Sleazy" "Slimy" "Scumbag"' (2 June 2008,
http://www.huffingtonpost.com/mayhill-fowler/bill-clinton-purdhum-a-sl_b_104771.html).
[92] *Guardian* (20 June 2008, www.guardian.co.uk/world/2008/jun/20/barackobama.uselections2008).
[93] 'When Mayhill Fowler Met Bill Clinton at the Rope Line' (9 June 2008,
http://journalism.nyu.edu/pubzone/weblogs/pressthink/2008/06/09/fowler_clinton.html). See also
'From Off the Bus to Meet the Press' (15 Apr. 2008,
http://journalism.nyu.edu/pubzone/weblogs/pressthink/2008/04/15/mayhill_fowler.html).

among Republicans) candidates had embraced social media tools as a way to mobilise grassroots support. For its part, the US mainstream media quickly partnered with entities such as MySpace and YouTube. YouTube invited Americans to upload questions they wanted the candidates to answer. More than 7,000 videos were uploaded and several were selected for two debates among the Democratic and Republican candidates that were broadcast on CNN. MySpace and MSNBC held a competition to select two users to send to the Democratic or Republican conventions, in an attempt to bring a 'new perspective to the news'.[94]

Blogs were seen by many as a way to sidestep the horse-race coverage of the traditional media and engage issues in a more substantive fashion. Was this the case, even discounting the clearly partisan stance that the most popular political blogs took? That's the question political scientist Mike Gruszczynski was interested in answering. He examined leading US political blogs, comparing the way they framed issues and wrote about candidates. He discovered that the political bloggers tended to 'dominate the narrative with their own voice, demonstrate clear tendencies toward punditry and editorializing, and exhibit extreme intra- and inter-party bias'. Gruszczynski wrote:

> *Though many may welcome the decline in gatekeeping ability of the mainstream media brought on by political blogs, the data presented here suggest that political blogs do not provide the American citizenry with a viable, healthy alternative to the long-entrenched mainstream media.*[95]

Usage

But what of actual usage? How many people are using this newfound ability—seen as a threat by some, an opportunity by others? Again, there is a lack of data but we can make a few broad observations.[96] According to a report by the American polling and market research firm Zogby International, while a majority of Americans (55 per cent) said bloggers are important to the future of American journalism, and 74 per cent said

---

[94] 'Citizen Journalists Make New Inroads into Political Reporting', *Christian Science Monitor* (28 July 2008).

[95] Gruszczynski, 'Comparing Apples and Blogs'.

[96] OECD, *Measuring User-Created Content*, 5: 'However, there is a lack of internationally comparable data on UCC from national statistical sources, and of knowledge on changing usage habits. As a result, it is often hard to accurately assess the statistical, economic, and societal effects of UCC and to devise appropriate policies.'

citizen journalism will play a vital role,[97] only 30 per cent of those surveyed ranked blogs as 'important' sources of news. This was well below websites (81 per cent), television (78 per cent), radio (73 per cent), newspapers (69 per cent) and magazines (38 per cent). According to Zogby: 'More Americans, 39%, chose friends and neighbors over blogs as an important informational source.'

A 2006 study by Sweden's Annika Bergström found that just 24 per cent of respondents thought that the ability to comment was 'important' or 'very important' to a news site on the web. This was above ads (22 per cent) and chat room (21 per cent) but well below the most highly rated attributes: continuously updated (98 per cent), easy to navigate (98 per cent), simple and clear (96 per cent) and free of cost (90 per cent).

Some 84 per cent of respondents had never commented on a news article, but the perceived value of commenting was important to some respondents, especially those arguably most likely not to engage with mainstream journalism. Those who described themselves as *not interested* in the news were more likely to comment than those *interested* in the news – 14 versus 9 per cent – and they were more likely to *perceive* an importance in being able to comment: 40 versus 24 per cent. Also, younger people were both more likely to think it important to comment and to *actually* comment. [98]

This, I think, is part of the key to citizen journalism's value: it appeals most to those the mainstream media is most at risk of losing. These are the people who characterise user-created content this way:

> *It is always available. It is fast. It is free. It is tuned to my interests, with none of the bullshit. They advertise to me less ... Stories can be discussed or debunked in the comment sections. Often, stories can be backed up with actual evidence, unlike a normal newspaper which will only tell you the story with a 'trust us' attitude ...*[99]

---

[97] Winter 2007 WE Media/Zogby Interactive poll (www.zogby.com/search/ReadNews.dbm?ID=1247). Note: the survey was conducted online using a method not embraced by the entire polling community.
[98] A. Bergström, 'The Reluctant Audience: Online Participation in the Swedish Journalistic Context' (Westminster Papers of Communication and Culture, forthcoming): 29% of 15–29 year olds were likely to think commenting was important while 18% actually commented. Also, while 5% of respondents interested in the news had blogs, 12% of those not interested in the news had blogs.
[99] Quoted in Wei, 'The Hype'.

The challenge for the mainstream media is to address this mindset. As Bill Kovach and Tom Rosenstiel write:

> *Journalists must invite their audience into the process by which they produce the news. They should take pains to makes themselves and their work as transparent as they insist on making the people and institutions of power they cover. This sort of approach is, in effect, the beginning of a new kind of connection between the journalist and the citizen.*[100]

[100] Bill Kovach and Tom Rosenstiel, *The Elements of Journalism: What Newspeople Should Know and the Public Should Expect* (Three Rivers Press, 2001), 191–2.

6. Where next? A few predictions

It would be interesting to see a large, mainstream, general-interest newspaper adhere to the old journalistic model—strong gatekeepers in place; few avenues for reader contribution—just as some sort of control experiment. We could then judge whether notions of brand, legitimacy and 'purity' trump those of openness and interactivity. I don't think any mainstream media outlet can afford to do that, however. The same technological and sociological changes that allow people to book their own airline tickets, post their own book reviews on Amazon.com, and upload their own videos to YouTube have forever altered the relationship they have with their news media.

It is impossible to foresee exactly how these changes will affect journalism, but here are some predictions for the next decade.

For a minority of people citizen journalism will provide an outlet for creativity, inquisitiveness and activism. The 'one percent rule' will apply: just 1 per cent of visitors to news websites will contribute content of some form. For most readers, it will be an avenue that is rarely used, more appreciated for the *opportunity* for interactivity than the actual use of that interactivity.

But this opportunity should not be underestimated. Readers will expect the mainstream media of 2010 to be more responsive than the mainstream media of 1990. Mainstream news outlets that neglect to allow their readers to participate will risk losing those readers. In a culture that increasingly views news as a commodity, users will look for differentiating factors as they choose their news sources. The quality and legitimacy of the product will be aspects—perhaps even the most important ones—but so too will be the extent to which the media responds to its customers and gives them useful tools to customize, share and contribute to the news. Furthermore, the openness with which the media deals with readers will determine how quickly and strongly it can repair its damaged reputation.

However, attempts to graft UGC into existing offerings merely as craven ploys to capture users' loyalty will be met with indifference or disdain. It will be better to restrict the ways readers can contribute—but to ensure those contributions can be made in a meaningful way—than to create Potemkin Villages of citizen journalism.

Even so, the greatest benefits of citizen journalism will accrue to the mainstream media outlets that employ it. For them, UGC will be a way to keep in near-constant touch with an audience that can function as a permanent focus group. It will also be a way to find sources quickly.

Improvements in reputation systems will address some of the misgivings editors have towards user-generated content. Pseudonymous commenting will be allowed, but mainstream media companies will require that all commenters be registered, with real names or e-mail addresses, so that those who repeatedly post offensive or defamatory material can be blocked. Users will appreciate this.

In its own way, it will be nearly as difficult to launch a successful stand-alone citizen journalism project in the network age as it was to launch a newspaper or television station in the broadcast age. The hurdles will not be expensive capital investments or complicated technological requirements but intense competition for what might be called intellectual capacity. The explosion of material on the web will make it harder for any single website to rise above the crowd.[101] In Anthony Lilley's words, we live in a time of 'infobesity', our finite attention spans overwhelmed by infinite information.[102]

Unique voices will rise above the din. These unique voices and images will surface during unique circumstances, most commonly aided by the same sort of media gatekeepers once accused of blocking diversity. Non-journalists who find themselves in newsworthy situations will turn to the

[101] For a counterintuitive take on this, see Fang Wu and Bernardo A. Huberman, 'Persistence and Success in the Information Economy'. They analysed the production histories and 'success dynamics' of 10 million YouTube videos submitted before 30 Apr. 2008. They found that 'the more frequently an individual uploads content the less likely it is that it will reach a success threshold. This paradoxical result is further compounded by the fact that the average quality of submissions does increase with the number of uploads, with the likelihood of success less than that of playing a lottery' (http://arxiv.org/abs/0904.0489).
[102] Anthony Lilley, 'Who Controls the Stories?', the first lecture by the News International Visiting Professor of Broadcast Media, delivered at Oxford University (15 Jan. 2008, see http://voxford.blogspot.com/search/label/Anthony%20Lilley). But see also Kevin Kawamoto (ed.), *Digital Journalism: Emerging Media and the Changing Horizons of Journalism* (Rowman & Littlefield, 2003): 'A self-regulated media diet puts control into the hands of the consumer of news, not the producer. A free and democratic society is better off risking information overload than risking information scarcity.'

BBC, CNN and other well-known players who have proven that they can widely distribute news. News that winds up in niche markets will be niche news, findable in the nether reaches of the long tail. But few people will believe that the long tail is where their news should be.

In retrospect, the early 'battles' over citizen journalism will cease to seem very important. Economic concerns will preoccupy editors and publishers. This will make it dangerous to invest in citizen journalism as a cost-saving measure, since true cost savings will prove illusory. Doubtless it will also cause some mainstream outlets to cut back on traditional forms of news gathering as they shift money to UGC and social media. Striking the right balance here—how lean can a news operation be before it ceases to be a credible news organization?—will be the central dilemma as we move from the broadcast age to the network age.

These are *journalistic* predictions, but what about *social* predictions? Just as citizen journalism is a subset of journalism, so the anxieties over its social impact will exist within larger concerns over the increasing atomisation of citizens—and of news consumers. By the early 21st century the shared experience of a daily newspaper as described by Benedict Anderson was already approaching the status of a historical artefact:

> [*Each*] *communicant is well aware that the ceremony he performs* [*reading that day's paper*] *is being replicated simultaneously by thousands (or millions) of others of whose existence he is confident, yet of whose identity he has not the slightest notion. Furthermore, this ceremony is incessantly repeated at daily or half-daily intervals throughout the calendar. ... At the same time, the newspaper reader, observing exact replicas of his own paper being consumed by his subway, barbershop or residential neighbors, is continually reassured that the imagined world is visibly rooted in every day.*[103]

The internet has uprooted the imagined world, or rather, it has created countless imagined worlds. This will threaten the monopoly of the traditional media, as the media competes with ever more narratives. Some of these narratives will be citizen-created. Their proponents will argue that the change this entails goes beyond mere journalism, that these are tools that can re-wire society. And yet, just as we must acknowledge that not every citizen wants to be a journalist, so we must accept that not every

---

[103] Benedict Anderson, *Imagined Communities: Reflections on the Origins and Spread of Nationalism* (Verso, 1991), 35.

citizen even wants to be a *citizen*, that is, a civically minded, actively participating member of a democracy. It is for that reason the new social landscape will likely resemble the old one in important respects. Those citizens most motivated to participate will be elites who would be involved in the political process regardless of the ease with which the mainstream media makes interactivity possible.

Questions for the future

Still, the field is wide open in terms of the need for further study. Among questions that should be asked are the following. How often do citizens engage with user-generated content as readers? What value do they place upon it? What do they contribute as creators and how often? How do user-generated material and the structure of citizen journalism sites differ from the mainstream media? What direction and at what speed and intensity does the news agenda flow? How has user-generated content changed that? What is the overlap between stories the news media deems important and those consumers deem important, examined in terms of reading online, forwarding and commenting? Can researchers demonstrate any difference in political awareness, political affiliation or political involvement between those who rely on the mainstream media and those who rely on a media diet heavy on citizen journalism? An even larger question is how does the newfound ability to make public our once-private experiences and thoughts change the way we perceive the public sphere?[104]

In the end, however, journalists must view user-generated content through a *journalistic* lens, not a sociological one. Does a certain element of it improve the overall journalism? If it does it should be encouraged. If it doesn't it is a distraction.

Which brings us back to that red kayak. After the story of John Darwin's miraculous return became news around the world a Panamanian woman named Patricia Centella de Lopez sent an email to the BBC's user-generated content hub. The Darwins, she wrote, had been her neighbours in Panama City. A television interview came from this contact, a connection that would have seemed unlikely in the pre-networked age.[105]

[104] See Benkler, *Wealth of Networks*, 213: 'The easy possibility of communicating effectively into the public sphere allows individuals to reorient themselves from passive readers and listeners to potential speakers and participants in a conversation. The way we listen to what we hear changes because of this; as does, perhaps most fundamentally, the way we observe and process daily events in our lives. We no longer need to take these as merely private observations, but as potential subjects for public communication. This changes the relative power of the media. It affects the structure of intake of observations and views.'
[105] http://news.bbc.co.uk/1/hi/england/tees/7131548.stm

'Sometimes, like this, there are gems that turn into on-air gold', reads the script of the user-generated content module presented by the BBC's in-house university, the corporation's attempt to harness citizen journalism. It is mining this gold—to present a more timely, accurate and compelling portrait of our world—that is citizen journalism's greatest promise.

Bibliography

Anderson, Chris, *The Long Tail: Why the Future of Business is Selling Less of More* (Hyperion, 2006).

Beckett, Charlie, *SuperMedia: Saving Journalism So it Can Save the World* (Blackwell Publishing, 2008).

Benkler, Y., *The Wealth of Networks: How Social Production Transforms Markets and Freedom* (Yale University Press, 2006).

Bentley, C., Meyer, H., and Littau, J., *Citizen Journalism and the TMC: User Content as a Driver for a Free Newspaper* (Association for Education in Journalism and Mass Communication, 2007).

Bowman, Shayne, and Willis, Chris, *We Media: How Audiences Are Shaping the Future of News and Information* (Media Center at the American Press Institute, 2003; pdf available at: www.hypergene.net/wemedia/weblog.php).

Bradshaw, Paul, 'Wiki Journalism: Are Wikis the New Blogs?', paper presented at the Future of Newspapers Conference, Cardiff, 2007.

Bruns, Axel, 'The Future is User-Led: The Path towards Widespread Produsage', presented at 'perthDAC 2007: The Future of Digital Media Culture', 7th International Digital Arts and Culture Conference (http://snurb.info/node/719).

Campbell, Vincent, Gibson, Rachel, Gunter, Barrie and Touri, Maria, 'News Blogs and the Future of Newspapers', paper presented at the Future of Newspapers Conference, Cardiff, 2007.

Carlson, Matt, 'Blogs and Journalistic Authority: The Role of Blogs in US Election Day 2004 Coverage', *Journalism Studies*, 8/2 (2007), 264–79.

Cooper, Glenda, 'Anyone Here Survived a Wave, Speak English and Got a Mobile? Aid Agencies, the Media and Reporting Disasters since the Tsunami', 14th Guardian Lecture, presented at Nuffield College, Oxford University, 2007.

Davies, Nick, *Flat Earth News* (Chatto & Windus, 2008).

Domingo, D., Quandt, T., Heinonen, A., Paulussen, S., Singer, J., and Vujnovic, M., 'Participatory Journalism Practices in the Media and Beyond: An International Comparative Study of Initiatives in Online Newspapers', paper presented at the Future of Newspapers Conference, Cardiff 2007.

Escher, Tobias, 'Bloggers with an Agenda: Developing a Methodology to Assess Whether Bloggers Rate Topics Independent from Media', Project Report for Social Research and the Internet, Oxford Internet Institute, Hillary 2007.

Gardam, Tim, and Levy, David (eds), *The Price of Plurality: Choice, Diversity and Broadcasting Institutions in the Digital Age* (Reuters Institute for the Study of Journalism/Ofcom, 2008).

Gillmor, Dan, *We the Media: Grassroots Journalism, by the People, for the People* (O'Reilly Media, 2006).

Hermida, Alfred, and Thurman, Neil, 'A Clash of Cultures: The Integration of User-Generated Content within Professional Journalistic Frameworks at British Newspaper Websites', *Journalism Practice*, 2/3 (2008), 343–56.

Kawamoto, Kevin (ed.), *Digital Journalism: Emerging Media and the Changing Horizons of Journalism* (Rowman & Littlefield Publishers, 2003).

Keen, Andrew, *The Cult of the Amateur: How the Democratization of the Digital World is Assaulting our Economy, our Culture, and our Values* (Currency/Doubleday, 2007).

Keller, Bill, 'Not Dead Yet: The Newspaper in the Days of Digital Anarchy', Hugo Young Memorial Lecture, delivered at Chatham House, 29 Nov. 2007 (www.guardian.co.uk/media/2007/nov/29/pressandpublishing.digitalmedia1).

Kline, David, and Burstein, Dan, *Blog! How the Newest Media Revolution is Changing Politics, Business, and Culture* (CDS Books, 2005).

Littau, Jeremy, 'Content Differences for an Online Newspaper Site and its Citizen Journalism Publication', paper presented to the Association for Education in Journalism and Mass Communication meeting, Washington, DC, 2007.

Lloyd, John, *What the Media are Doing to our Politics* (Constable. 2004).

Lloyd, Levon, Kaulgud, Prachi, and Skiena, Steven, 'Newspapers vs. Blogs: Who Gets the Scoop?', paper presented at the 2006 Association for the Advancement of Artificial Intelligence, Spring Symposium Technical Report SS-06-03 (AAAI Press, Menlo Park, CA).

Maier, Michael, 'Journalism without Journalists: Vision or Caricature?' Discussion paper #D-40 in the Joan Shorenstein Center on the Press, Politics and Public Policy series, John F. Kennedy School of Government, Harvard University, Nov. 2007.

Monck, Adrian, with Hanley, Mike, *Can You Trust the Media?* (Icon Books, 2008).

National Union of Journalists, 'Shaping the Future: Commission on Multi-Media Working', Dec. 2007.

Nip, J., 'Exploring the Second Phase of Public Journalism', *Journalism Studies*, 7/2 (Apr. 2006), 213–36.

Paulussen, Steve, Heinonen, Ari, Domingo, David, and Quandt, Thorsten, 'Doing it Together: Citizen Participation in the Professional News Making Process', paper presented at the COST 298 Conference 'The Good, the Bad and the Unexpected: The User and Future of Information and Communication Technologies', 23–25 May 2007, Moscow.

Reich, Zvi, 'A Matter of Accessibility: Comparing the Sourcing Practices of Citizen and Mainstream Journalists', Paper presented at the Future of Newspapers Conference, Cardiff, 2007.

Ryfe, David, and Mensing, Donica, 'Doing Journalism Together: Experiments in Collaborative Newsgathering', paper presented at the Future of Newspapers Conference, Cardiff, 2007.

Scanlon, Sean, 'News as Conversation: How Newspapers are Responding to New Media and the Implications for New Zealand', Reuters Institute for the Study of Journalism, Paper 279, Trinity 2006.

Schaffer, Jan, 'Citizen Media: Fad or the Future of News?', Knight Citizens News Network, 2007 (www.kcnn.org/research/citizen_media_report).

Schlesinger, David, 'Journalism in the Age of Innovation', lecture to the Reuters Institute for the Study of Journalism, Oxford, 2007.

Schweiger, Wolfgang, and Quiring, Oliver, 'User-Generated Content on Mass Media Web Sites: Just a Kind of Interactivity or Something Completely Different?', paper presented to the 55th annual conference of the International Communication Association, New York, 2005.

Surowiecki, James, *The Wisdom of Crowds: Why the Many are Smarter than the Few* (Doubleday, 2004).

Thurman, Neil, 'Forums for Citizen Journalists? Adoption of User Generated Content Initiatives by Online News Media', *New Media and Society*, 10/1 (2008), 139–57.

Ugille, Pieter, and Paulussen, Steve, 'Moderation, Conversation and Collaboration? Organisational Implications of Citizen Journalism Projects in Professional Newsrooms', paper presented at the Future of Newspapers Conference, Cardiff, 2007.

Wardle, Claire, and Williams, Andrew, 'UGC @ the BBC: Understanding its Impact upon Contributors, Non-Contributors and BBC News', Cardiff University report to the BBC Knowledge Exchange Programme and the Arts and Humanities Research Council, 16 Sept. 2008 (www.bbc.co.uk/blogs/knowledgeexchange/cardiffone.pdf).

Wei, Hsing, 'The Hype vs. Reality vs. What People Value: Emerging Collaborative News Models and the Future of News', masters project, Spring 2006, John F. Kennedy School of Government, Harvard University (http://citmedia.org/learn/surveys/collaborativenews.htm).

Acknowledgements

I am grateful to the Reuters Institute for the Study of Journalism for allowing me the luxury of a year in Oxford to think about journalism without actually having to produce it. My thanks to Sarmila Bose, then-director of the institute, for accepting me as a visiting fellow, to David Levy, the institute's current director, for his energy and his interest in my project, to director of journalism John Lloyd for his penetrating journalistic conscience, and to Colin Bundy, president of what is now Green Templeton College, for the hospitality he showed to all the Reuters Fellows. I must also thank Leonard Downie, former executive editor of *The Washington Post*, who, when I first mentioned I wanted to take a sabbatical from the paper, suggested the Reuters Institute, and Paddy Coulter, who was open and encouraging to my early enquiries. The institute staff, including Rima Dapous, Kate Hanneford-Smith and Trevor Mostyn, helped make my year an enjoyable one.

Many journalists and academics were gracious enough to talk with me and welcome me into their domains. Thanks especially to Vicky Taylor of the BBC's UGC Hub, Telegraph Communities Editor Shane Richmond, Charlie Beckett of POLIS at the London School of Economics, Henrik Ornebring of the Reuters Institute, Adrian Monck of City University, Tim Gardam of St Anne's College, David Butler of Nuffield College, and John Naughton of the Wolfson Press Fellowship Programme in that other academic town, Cambridge. Some of these people are in different jobs now but I don't think that had anything to do with meeting me.

Thomson Reuters deserves an expression of gratitude for making it possible for ink-, videotape-, audiotape- and pixel-stained wretches from around the world to gather in that most sublime of cities. It is hard to describe the positive knock-on effect of spending so much time with such a diverse group of fellow journalists. To a person the fellows I met at the Reuters Institute were friendly, intelligent and committed to safely transporting the spirit of journalism through these difficult times. In particular I'd like to thank Richard Danbury, Glenda Cooper, Kenneth Payne, Meera Jeevan and Malcolm Dean for many hours of thought-provoking conversation. Not long after I turned in my first draft of this paper, my computer hard-drive failed. Fortunately, I had emailed a copy to another fellow Abel Escudero Zadrayec. I thank him for sending it back to me so I didn't have to start again totally from scratch.

The practice of ending the acknowledgements with the statement that any errors of fact or judgement are the author's alone has always struck me as an unnecessary cliché and yet I feel compelled to follow suit.

Washington, 1 June 2009